A CLIENT'S POINT OF VIEW

EXCERPTS FROM: WRIT OF CERTIORARI:

A CLIENT'S POINT OF VIEW

EXCERPTS FROM: WRIT OF CERTIORARI:

By

SONIA V. GRANT.

1stbooks Rev. 09/03/00

ABOUT THE BOOK

"A Client's Point of View" is a compilation of court documents that presents how one woman's home in New York City may have been erroneously demolished and subsequent hearings and trials. It relates the proceedings of the city and state courts on civil lawsuits with personal accounts. The narrative and filing papers describe dramatic and emotional trauma of returning to a home that no longer stands and the loss of all its contents. This compelling story takes you down the road of optimism, enthusiasm, and the ultimate disappointment.

INTRODUCTION

This is a story about a Case between Sonia Grant, plaintiff-Appellant and The In Rem Release Board, Mayor, City of New York et al . . . . ., and a Construction Co., Respondents.

About three years ago: On or about, May 24, 1993, Respondents wrongly destroyed Plaintiff's house and all belongings, everything that she owned. Respondents made a mistake with the Block and Lot numbers.

Today, Respondents have left bad structural damages.

Plaintiff brought suit against Respondents several days later, in the Supreme Court of the State of New York, Brooklyn N.Y., Though at the time, Plaintiff was emotionally distraught. On March 3rd 1994, a decision was made, that, even though her case was compelling, a judgement went for the Respondents; Plaintiff further took her Case to a Higher Court, the New York State Supreme Court, Appellate Division - Second Department, Brooklyn N.Y.

Plaintiff has overwhelming arguments to win her case and to become vindicated. She seeks the following relief: (a) Prevent the City from performing construction on the Subject Property. (b) Convey Title to Plaintiff. (c) Money Damages in the amount of $50 Million. (d) Any other relief the Court may deem proper.

Her Case was callendered to be heard in the Appellate Court, Brooklyn N.Y. that Friday, February 23, 1996 at 10 a.m.

Case No.

CHAPTER ONE

Gertrude spent most of her teenage life in New York. She had many ambitions. She wanted to make it in New York. Her biggest desires were to own a home and to have a successful business. As Gertrude grew older, she saw many sides of the inner city both good and bad. Some of the obstacles made Gertrude stronger. Despite the adversities of a big city she pursued her wishes. She saved up her pennies until she acquired a large enough sum.In 1985, Gertrude purchased a home in a City Auction. It was a brownstone house on the Parkway, in Brooklyn, nearby Atlantic Avenue. The house needed to be renovated. After renovation, Gertrude moved into her house. Neighbors welcomed her and they were amazed at her house. She began to like her new neighborhood. Soon she would get accustomed to the bustling noise of the traffic all year round. Except when it was Carnival on the Parkway, it was the noise of the vendors, the rattling of the steel bands and the millions of people as they came together for their festivity. Gertrude loved carnivals and she saw her house as part of the program. From the top level of her house she could see beautiful costumes, colorful sequins and glitter shining in the street. People in the bands wearing masks and dancing on the trucks. The most funniest, is how sometimes they throw glitter, white powder and spray water on spectators. Gertrude used to join in with some of bands, but not anymore. Instead she eats plenty of food, pick on tasty fish, and festival and she washes it down with delicious cold, icy fruit punch or soda. From her loft she could view famous marchers and politicians parading on the stands, as they waved to prospective voters.

So every year during the fall season, she collected various pieces, ornaments, paintings that she planned to put on display in her loft for the next year's carnival. But this particular Summer was unusual. Gertrude was determined to start her own business. As time went on Gertrude kept putting it off. "Maybe I'll be ready next carnival", she said. Several months later, she began to encounter a land problem with government. The following Spring, Gertrude's house was destroyed. When Gertrude returned home that day she found contractors demolishing her house. Faint and hostile as she was, she filed a lawsuit in the Supreme Court in Brooklyn, against the City of New York and a Contracting Company. The caption reads, Sonia Grant, Plaintiff, against the City of New York, Mayor, In Rem Release Board et al respondents. Gertrude, the pet name for the Plaintiff, now began to pursue her lawsuit. However, in March 1994, Plaintiff lost her battle with the "City" in the lower courts. She continued her case when she appealed to the New York Supreme Court, Appellate Division Second Department.

In November 1994, After various proceedings in the Appellate Court, relating to poor person status, Plaintiff still proceeding prose, perfected her appeal.

PARALIZED

by: Gertrude

Brick by Brick It was built on hopes
and dreams.
It could have been a day care center
or a flower shop.
And now those hopes have
come to an unnecessary stop.
Brick by Brick it was destroyed
like shattered sun beams.

In a matter of minutes its existence
was forgotten.
Second by Second anything It could have ever
become, crumbled.
The evil villains that diminished its world,
Is extremely despised
Second by Second its structure quickly,
hit rock bottom.

Hopefully, It will be rebuilt and given
another chance.

The end.

SUPREME COURT OF THE STATE OF NEW YORK

APPELLATE DIVISION : SECOND DEPARTMENT

April 25, 1994

Sonia Grant

A file has been opened in the case of:

TITLE: Grant v In Rem Release Board
COURT: Supreme   COUNTY: Kings PAPER: Order
DATED: 03/03/94   INDEX NO.:

This case has been assigned the following number on the dock this court:

ALL PAPERS AND CORRESPONDENCE RELATING TO THIS MATTER MUST HEREAFTER BEAR THIS CASE NUMBER.

Clerk

Form A - Request for Appellate Division Intervention - Civil

See § 670.3 of the rules of this court for directions on the use of this form (22 NYCRR 670.3).

Case Title. Set forth the title of the case as it appears on the summons, notice of petition or order to show cause by which the matter was or is to be commenced, or as amended:

Sonia Grant

~against~ (Petitioner)

In Rem Release Board, (Respondents)
David N. Dinkins, Mayor, City of New York
Peter Vallone, Speaker, Corporation Council,
Commissioner of Finance Borough
President, Housing Preservation and
Development, Felice Mischetti (Commissioner
Housing Preservation and Development)
Construction Company.

For Court of Original Instance

Date Notice of Appeal Filed

For Appellate Division

Case Type		Filing Type	
☐ Civil Action	☐ CPLR article 78 Proceeding	☐ Appeal	☐ Transferred Proceeding
☐ CPLR article 75 Arbitration	☐ Special Proceeding Other	☐ Original Proceeding	☐ CPLR 5704 Review
	☐ Habeas Corpus Proceeding		

Nature of Suit: Check up to five of the following categories which best reflect the nature of the case.

A. Administrative Review	D. Domestic Relations	F. Prisoners	I. Torts
☐ 1 Freedom of Information Law	☐ 1 Adoption	☐ 1 Discipline	☐ 1 Assault, Battery, False
☑ 2 Human Rights	☐ 2 Attorney's Fees	☐ 2 Jail Time Calculation	Imprisonment
☐ 3 Licenses	☐ 3 Children - Support	☐ 3 Parole	☐ 2 Conversion
☐ 4 Public Employment	☐ 4 Children - Custody/Visitation	☐ 4 Other	☐ 3 Defamation
☐ 5 Social Services	☐ 5 Children - Terminate Parent-		☑ 4 Fraud
☑ 6 Other	al Rights	**G. Real Property**	☐ 5 Intentional Infliction of
	☐ 6 Children - Abuse/Neglect	☐ 1 Condemnation	Emotional Distress
B. Business & Other Relationships	☐ 7 Children - JD/PINS	☑ 2 Determine Title	☐ 6 Interference with Contract
☐ 1 Partnership/Joint Venture	☐ 8 Equitable Distribution	☐ 3 Easements	☐ 7 Malicious Prosecution/
☐ 2 Business	☐ 9 Exclusive Occupancy of	☐ 4 Environmental	Abuse of Process
☐ 3 Religious	Residence	☐ 5 Liens	☐ 8 Malpractice
☐ 4 Not-for-Profit	☐ 10 Expert's Fees	☐ 6 Mortgages	☑ 9 Negligence
☑ 5 Other	☐ 11 Maintenance/Alimony	☐ 7 Partition	☐ 10 Nuisance
	☐ 12 Marital Status	☐ 8 Rent	☐ 11 Products Liability
C. Contracts	☐ 13 Paternity	☐ 9 Taxation	☐ 12 Strict Liability
☐ 1 Brokerage	☐ 14 Spousal Support	☐ 10 Zoning	☑ 13 Trespass and/or Waste
☐ 2 Commercial Paper	☐ 15 Other	☐ 11 Other	☐ 14 Other
☑ 3 Construction			
☐ 4 Employment	**E. Miscellaneous**	**H. Statutory**	**J. Wills & Estates**
☐ 5 Insurance	☐ 1 Constructive Trust	☐ 1 City of Mount Vernon	☐ 1 Accounting
☑ 6 Real Property	☐ 2 Debtor & Creditor	Charter §§ 120, 127-f, or	☐ 2 Discovery
☐ 7 Sales	☐ 3 Declaratory Judgment	129	☐ 3 Probate/Administration
☐ 8 Secured	☐ 4 Election Law	☐ 2 Eminent Domain Proced-	☐ 4 Trusts
☐ 9 Other	☑ 5 Notice of Claim	ure Law § 207	☐ 5 Other
	☑ 6 Other	☐ 3 General Municipal Law	
		§ 712	
		☐ 4 Labor Law § 220	
		☐ 5 Public Service Law §§ 128	
		or 170	
		☐ 6 Other	

5

Paper Appealed From (check one only):

☐ Amended Decree ☐ Determination ☑ Order ☐ Resettled Order
☐ Amended Judgment ☐ Finding ☐ Order & Judgment ☐ Ruling
☐ Amended Order ☐ Interlocutory Decree ☐ Partial Decree ☐ Other (specify):
☐ Decision ☐ Interlocutory Judgment ☐ Resettled Decree
☐ Decree ☐ Judgment ☐ Resettled Judgment

Court: _Supreme Court of State of N.Y._ County: _Kings_

Dated: _March 2nd 1994_ Entered: _March 15th 1994_

Judge (name in full): ___ Index No.: _17342/93_

Stage: ☐ Interlocutory ☐ Final ☑ Post-Final Trial: ☐ Yes ☑ No If Yes: ☐ Jury ☐ Non-Jury

Prior Unperfected Appeal Information

Are any unperfected appeals pending in this case? ☐ Yes ☐ No. If yes, do you intend to perfect the appeal or appeals covered by the annexed notice of appeal with the prior appeals? ☐ Yes ☐ No. Set forth the Appellate Division Cause Number(s) of any prior, pending, unperfected appeals:

Original Proceeding

Commenced by: ☐ Order to Show Cause ☑ Notice of Petition ☐ Writ of Habeas Corpus Date Filed: _May 25th 1993_

Statute authorizing commencement of proceeding in the Appellate Division:

Proceeding Transferred Pursuant to CPLR 7804(g)

Court: ___ County: ___

Judge (name in full): ___ Order of Transfer Date: ___

CPLR 5704 Review of Ex Parte Order

Court: ___ County: ___

Judge (name in full): ___ Dated: ___

Description of Appeal, Proceeding or Application and Statement of Issues

Description: If an appeal, briefly describe the paper appealed from. If the appeal is from an order, specify the relief requested and whether the motion was granted or denied. If an original proceeding commenced in this court or transferred pursuant to CPLR 7804(g), briefly describe the object of the proceeding. If an application under CPLR 5704, briefly describe the nature of the ex parte order to be reviewed.

Appeal from an Order with Notice of Settlement.
Petitioner request for an Order compelling respondents to convey title to certain real property back to her and for money damages in the amount of $50M. Respondents move to deny Plaintiff's Petition. Petitioner's request was denied.

Amount: If an appeal is from a money judgment, specify the amount awarded.

Issues: Specify the issues proposed to be raised on the appeal, proceeding, or application for CPLR 5704 review.

Notice of Claim was filed - July 28th 1993.
Respondents, wrongfully demolish Petitioner's house; negligence, trespass, destruction, emotional distress and personal injuries; defacto condemnation of real and personal property.

Petitioner further contends that her human rights were violated;

SUPREME COURT OF THE STATE OF NEW YORK

APPELLATE DIVISION : SECOND JUDICIAL DEPARTMENT

------------------------------------X

SONIA GRANT,

                    Plaintiff, Appellant

    -against-   MOTION OF

                                                 PREFERENCE

IN REM RELEASE **BOARD,**
MAYOR, CITY OF NEW YORK, et al.,   App. Div. Case No.
                                        Index No.

                    Respondents.

------------------------------------X

    Sirs:

    Please take Notice that, Plaintiff, Appellant, in this case,
will move this Court, at the Courthouse, Brooklyn, New York on
the 7th day of September 1995, at 9:30 O'clock in the fore-noon
or as soon thereafter as Counsel can be heard for a preference
in the above captioned case, under CPLR 5521; providing good
cause shown by this motion; that the above captioned case is a
Disaster Emergency and that Appellant in this case have not
received any aid in restoring my house or my life; and that it
has been over two years that the defendants in this case have
wrongfully destroyed Appellant's house; destroying all of my
belongings without any notice: and that the, Appellant, in this
case, seek for the Defendants, in this case to be brought to
Justice:

7

I, seek for an immediate or early trial, so that this case can be settled; so that Appellant can be vindicated and awarded.

Wherefore, Appellant bear these statements to be true, and for an order to move for the following relief:

a) To stop construction and excavation on the subject property.

b) Specific Performance i.e. The City to Convey Title to Appellant.

c) To seek money damages in the amount of $50 million.

d) Any other relief to this Court may deem proper.

Dated: New York, New York.
   August 18, 1995.

CHAPTER TWO

SUPREME COURT OF THE STATE OF NEW YORK
APPELLATE DIVISION - SECOND JUDICIAL DEPARTMENT

_____x

SONIA GRANT,

                Plaintiff-Appellant,

                  - against -   MOTION TO

                                    STRIKE THE

IN REM RELEASE BOARD,   BRIEF.

MAYOR,

CITY OF NEW YORK, et al.,

                                    Case No.

                Respondents-Respondents.

_____x

Sirs:

   Please take Notice that, Plaintiff, Appellant, in this case, move this Court, at the Courthouse, Brooklyn, New York 11201 to Strike Respondents' Brief; providing good cause shown in this motion.

   Plaintiff- Appellant, perfected her brief on November 18, 1994, and set forth in her brief overwhelming evidence and facts to support her case. Respondents' Brief of December 18, 1995 is untimely: Lack of proper evidence and facts, fairness, and a Breech of the Statue of Limitations.

Respondents, after wrongfully demolishing Plaintiff- Appellant's house, took over one year to Respond to my brief. Respondents should not use Statue of limitations to mock the Court, instead should look into this case with due respect and seriousness. Respondents had more than sufficient time to reply to my brief, of November 18, 1994; which shows on Respondents' Dart; guilt, a lack of concern and seriousness towards my case. In Addition, the Court would have had sufficient time to Calendar my case by now.

Therefore,   Plaintiff- Appellant,
am asking the Court to strike Respondents' Brief;

Wherefore,   Plaintiff-Appellant,
bear these statements to be true; and ask that my
Motion be granted.

                                Yours, respectfully,

                        _____

                        SONIA GRANT. (PRO SE)

Dated: New York, New York.
January 22, 1996.

SUPREME CCURT OF THE STATE OF NEW YORK

APPELLATE DIVISION: SECOND DEPARTMENT.

In the Matter of the Application of

   Sonia Grant,   Case. No.

                    Plaintiff- Appellant,

       -against-

In Rem Release Board, Mayor,

City of New York, et. al. respondents

.

Statement Under Rule 5531

1. The index Number assigned in the Court below

2. The full names of the original parties are set forth above. There has been no change of parties since the commencement of this action.

3. This special proceeding was commenced in Supreme Court of the State of New York.

4. This special proceeding was commenced by the Service of a Notice of Petition and Petition on or about May 25, 1993. Respondent's Verified Answer and Return was served on or about June 20, 1993.

5. The nature and object of this special proceeding pursuant to CPLR Article 78 was to challenge the right of the City to construct upon and / or excavate the subject property, to compel the City of New York to convey title to the property to Plaintiff and for money damages.

6. The Court below determined that this determination was not arbitrary or capricious nor was it an abuse of discretion.

7. The appeal is on full reproduced record.

8. The determination to be reviewed was rendered after reading the notice of cross-motions and after due deliberation having been held thereon.

Plaintiff and her family still suffers loss and
injuries of personal and property damages, bereavement
and emotional distress.

Plaintiff seeks, a) prevent the City from
performing construction on the Subject Property.
b) Convey Title to Plaintiff. c) money damages in the
amount of $50 Million. d) Any other relief to this Court
may deem proper.

Discussion and Conclusion.
Should Plaintiff be entitled to have a fair and just trial

It is fair to say, that historically, the Courts have been
silent and inactive in certain reform process, Society has great
confidence in the statutes and uniform acts and many of them
have done much good.

A specific tool of reform.

While various tools exist for improving the world of trusts and estates, my argument is about reading into all instruments rules that are useful and modern, and finding them in all trusts, whether the grantor put them there or not.

The topic, then is statutes and cases that help reach wise results

Analogically, For example, Some people call default rules off the rack rules or off the shelf rules. Just as the intestate succession statute provides a free will for people who do not make a will,

In civil law; the law of trusts and estates is a world in which the state provides a resolution for everyone. This system of laws is not new, except for the expression "default rule" and the tendancy to find a default rule behind every tree,

What is rather new is the academic insistence that the default rules be good. For example, Silence and Failure of Default rules; when dealing with the testator or the settlor who was silent, however what does silence mean? This silence might mean that the settlor said 'I trust the law to deal with the question;' I trust the law to operate in a way that is fair, impartial, efficient, normal, standard, and enlightened,

Unfortunately, Some courts act mindlessly because the "law" requires it. The law also requires balance, proportion, compassion and decency. Judges should refer to these concerns more often when reaching their decisions.

When society, through the courts, looks at the question of fiduciary Administration, it should not be a fuzzy

We should give the settlor what she must have wanted, that which is up-to-date and useful.

_____Sonia, Grant, PROSE_____

Appellant_____ .

MOTION FOR PERMISSION
TO APPEAL TO THE
COURT OF APPEALS

V.

Index No. _____
County K̶I̶N̶G̶S̶

In Rem Release Board, David N. Dinkins,
Mayor, City of New York et al.,
_____ Respondents

i. This Motion for Permission to Appeal to the Court of Appeals is being made by
_____ _ Prose, Appellant . _____ , __ ;

The return date is _____ .

ii. The questions presented for Court of Appeals review are:

1. Whether through intentional fraud and illegality, respondents unlawfully confiscated appellants property and violated appellant's human and constitutional rights?
2. Whether respondents are liable for negligence, trespass, destruction and wrongful demolition of Plaintiff's property?
3. Whether the actions taken by respondents were in conformity of the law?
4. Whether respondents are liable to the State of New York?
5. Whether its a matter of race?
6. Whether appellant has the right to a fair trial?

iii. The order which I am appealing was (circle one) (mailed) personally served upon me by the opposing party with notice of entry on April 1, 1996 .
(A copy of this order and opinion must be attached to these papers)

If you made a motion for permission to this Court in the Appellate Division, you must complete the statements in the box and attach a copy of the order denying your motion with notice of entry to these papers. If no such motion was first made in the Appellate Division go to paragraph iv on the next page.

the date that I (circle one) mailed/
personally served the Appellate Division motion
upon the opposing side was May 24, 1996/ August 30, 1996

the date that the Appellate Division order
denying the motion and notice of its entry
were (circle one) mailed/personally served upon me by the opposing party was
May 3, 1996 / October 2, 1996

17

iv. The Court of Appeals has jurisdiction to review this order because

Respondents violated appellant's human and constitutional rights, through constructive, intentional fraud and illegality. The lower court's decision to dismiss the entire case was erroneous. The Appellate court's decision affirming lower court's decision was also erroneous and wrong.

v. The Court of Appeals should accept this case for review because

The Appellate Court's decision Seems wrong as it overlooked or misapprehended the facts or law, overlooked by the lower court. The Appellate Court overlooked and misinterpreted that portion of fact and law in appellant's suit. The Appellate's Courts decision is erroneous and wrong. Appellant's arguments with respect regarding destruction of real property and infliction of emotional distress and damages, raised within days of the destruction of the building in which appellant was living, was raised both in the lower court and in the Appellate court is a result of the impact of respondents fraud and illegality

(use additional sheets if necessary)

CHAPTER THREE

OPINIONS BELOW

JURISDICTION ....

CONSTITUTIONAL AND STATUTORY PROVISIONS INVOLVED ....

STATEMENT OF THE CASE ....

REASONS FOR GRANTING THE WRIT.............................

CONCLUSION...

INDEX TO APPENDICES

APPENDIX A   Decision of State Court of Appeals

APPENDIX B   Decision of State Supreme Court - Appellate Division

APPENDIX C   Order of State Supreme Court Granting Summary
              Judgment

SUPREME COURT OF THE UNITED STATES

OCTOBER TERM, 1996

No. 1

PETITION FOR WRIT OF CERTIORARI

Petitioner respectfully prays that a writ of certiorari issue to review the judgment below.

OPINIONS BELOW

[ ] For cases from federal courts:

The opinion of the United States court of appeals appears at Appendix _____ to the petition and is

[ ] reported at _____; or,
[ ] has been designated for publication but is not yet reported; or,
[ ] is unpublished.

The opinion of the United States district court appears at Appendix _____ to the petition and is

[ ] reported at _____; or,
[ ] has been designated for publication but is not yet reported; or,
[ ] is unpublished.

[ ] For cases from state courts:

The opinion of the highest state court to review the merits appears at Appendix _____ to the petition and is

[ ] reported at _____; or,
[√] has been designated for publication but is not yet reported; or,
[√] is unpublished.

The opinion of the STATE OF NEW YORK court of Appeals appears at Appendix A to the petition and is

[ ] reported at _____; or,
[ ] has been designated for publication but is not yet reported; or,
[ ] is unpublished.

Question (s) Presented

Whether petitioner is a victim of discrimination, redlining and empowerment zoning; and whether respondents discriminated against petitioner, by targeting and redlining petitioner's property because of her race, and or sex?

Whether respondents are liable for negligence, trespass, malicious destruction and wrongful demolition of petitioner's property?

Question (s) Presented

Whether respondents violate petitioners human, civil and constitutional rights?

Whether respondents misrepresent taxation; and whether respondents abuse it's power?

Whether respondents sold petitioner a defective parcel? (as in respondents letter 10-29-90.)

Whether respondents constructively, intentionally and fraudulently violated petitioner's rights, and whether respondents denied petitioner her rights to the return of her property?

Whether repondents unlawfully discriminated against petitioner because of race and, or sex (petitioner is black and woman.)

Whether respondents intentionally, violently and unlawfully destroyed and conviscated petitioner's property; causing physical, mental, emotional injury and distress to petitioner?

REASONS FOR GRANTING THE PETITION

THE SUPREME COURT OF THE STATE OF NEW YORK,
Appellate Division: SECOND DEPARTMENT; Court that last ruled on
the merits of my case.   This court decided petitioner's appeal
by order dated April 1, 1996.   In order dated April 1, 1996,
Court affirmed the granting of summary judgement to respondents
on the basis of the lower court's decision.   Court erred in
granting of summary judgment to respondents.

The lower Court seemed wrong as it overlooked or misapprehended
the matter of facts or law presented in this case.   Because the
lower court addressed only those equitable claims recognizable
on an Article 78 proceeding and failed to address any
petitioner's legal claims for monetary damages.   Its decision to
dismiss the entire case was erroneous.   For the same reason, The
Appellate Court's decision affirming the lower Court's decision
was also erroneous.

CONSTITUTIONAL AND STATUTORY PROVISION INVOLVED

Article III Case:

Litigate seeking to establish Article III case or controversy must clearly demonstrate that he suffered injury in fact, that is concrete on both qualitative and temporal sense......and, is likely to be redressed by favorable decision. (Whitmore v Arkansas, U.S. Ark. 1990, 110 S. Ct. 1717, 465 U.S. 149, 109 L. Ed. 2d 135)

To have standing to seek injunctive relief under Article III, petitioner must demonstrate that she is likely to suffer fatal injury,......and that relief which she seeks will prevent injury from occurring......(Petitioner contends that:)Schlosser v. Coleman, M.D. Fla 1993, 818 F. Supp. 1534.

Latino and African-American neighborhood residents and organization composed of individuals and groups residing in neighborhood had standing to maintain suits alleging violation of their constitutional rights in connection......; plaintiff lived in neighborhood where disputed land sales took place and claimed they were being displaced......and complaint traced the alleged injury to City's actions including sale of property. (South side Fair Housing Committee v. City of New York, C.A. 2(NY) 1991, 928 F 2d 1336.) Mich. App 1976. Where defendants were attempting to prove that actual agreement contemplated......Agreement fell within Statue of Frauds, and memorandum was required. M.C.L.A. Sec. 566 108-Michigan Nat. Bank of Detroit v. Holland-Dazier Holland Sound Studios, 250 N.W. 2d 532, 73 Mich. App. 12.

CONSTITUTIONAL AND STATUTORY PROVISIONS INVOLVED

Petitioner's claims in tort do not depend on her status with respect to the property. Whether she was the owner of the property, a tenant, a license, or even a trespasser, the City owed her a duty not to inflict intentional harm on her or her property. Given her open and assertive residence in the property, the City's destruction of it, without giving her sufficient notice to remove her property was actionable as in intentional, or perhaps, as negligent destruction of her personal property, and as intentional, or perhaps, as negligent infliction of emotional distress. *See Nieves v. 331 East 109th Street Corp.* 112 A.D. 2d 59 (1st Dep't 1985) C.F. friends of Yelverton v. 163rd Street Improvement Council, 135 Misc. 2d 275 (Civ. Ct. Bronx County 1986)(even where no landlord tenant relationship existed, City's resort to self-help was illegal). Instead, the respondents' destruction of property left plaintiff without a place to live and without any of her property. No notice to quit, pursuant to real property actions and proceedings law sections 712 and 735 was even served upon petitioner.

REASONS FOR GRANTING THE PETITION

Whether respondents discriminated against petitioner, be single in out, targeting petitioner's home for demolition, and whether the actions taken by respondents were lawful, whether respondents abused, violated petitioner's human, civil and constitutional rights, and displacing?

The Court below did not address that portion of petitioner's suit that sought monetary damages.

Whether respondents are liable for destroying Petitioner's home, causing personal, severe emotional injury inflicted upon petitioner?

Whether there is a conflict of interest between "the City" and Construction Co. Incorporated to demolish petitioner's home, thereby displacing Petitioner; (Southside Fair Housing Committee v. City of New York, CA 2 (NY) 1441, 928 F 2d 1336)

CHAPTER FOUR

SUPREME COURT

OF UNITED STATES

_____X

Sonia Grant,

Petitioner,   AFFIRMATION IN

      V.   SUPPORT OF

In Rem Release Board et al.,   PETITION FOR

    Construction Co., Inc.   REHEARING.

        Respondents.   No. 96-8803

_____X

ARGUMENT

THE LOWER COURT,   IN GRANTING SUMMARY

JUDGEMENT, AND THE APPELLATE COURT,

IN AFFIRMING THE LOWER COURTS DECISION,

OVERLOOKED THAT PORTION OF PETITIONER'S

SUIT SEEKING MONETARY DAMAGES IN TORT.

In Petitioner's suit, petitioner originally sought the return

of real estate pursuant to the City's redemption procedures (see

N.Y.C. Admin. Code 11- 424 et seq.), monetary damages for

destruction of the building on that property, and monetary

damages for destruction of the building on that property, and

monetary damages for destruction of her personal property and

28

for infliction of emotional distress based on the demolition of the house in which she was living. Because there are factual issues in dispute relating to petitioner's tort claims, and those claims exist independently of the claims cognizant in Article 78 proceedings. Summary judgement in the lower court should not have been granted. Therefore, rehearing should be granted, the Lower court's decision granting summary judgement to the City and Construction Co. should be reversed, and the case should be remitted for rehearing.

The rehearing for petition is proper where a court "overlooked or misapprehended the facts or law or for reason mistakenly arrived at its earlier decision." Swenning v. Wankel, 140 A.D. 2d 428 (2d Dep't 1988). Moreover, a petition for rehearing is proper where the moving party alleges new facts. Petitioner raised issues of fact that are substantial to withstand a petition for rehearing. Refer to Rule 44, SUPREME COURT OF THE UNITED STATES.

Petitioner's petition for the rehearing is substantial to establish a claim in tort, or at least to alert the court and the respondents of a claim in tort, regardless of the validity of petitioner's claims with respect to her ownership of the building. Even assuming, but not conceding, that the city was the lawful owner of the building and that petitioner had no rights as the owner, petitioner still should have been free from the gratuitous destruction of personal property within the building. Instead, no need for quick action, as of the present, July 1997, the lot is still empty. The forcible destruction of petitioner's property entitled petitioner to recovery of treble damages pursuant to Real Property Actions and Proceedings Law Section 853 (Action for forcible or unlawful entry or

Whether petitioner was the owner of the property, a tenant, a licensee, or even a trespasser, the City owed petitioner a duty not to inflict intentional harm on petitioner or petitioner's property.

Finally, there is no evidence that a number 1455 Eastern Parkway existed.

Petitioner believes that there is a conflict of interest,

Also did the City sold the petitioner a defective property?

In sum, petitioner raises substantial grounds in her petition for rehearing, even with respect to petitioner's claims in tort. The lower court therefore erred in granting summary judgement to respondents and dismissing the entire suit. The Appellate's Court's decision did not consider the propriety of the lower court's decision as it pertained to petitioner's tort claims. By granting a petition for the rehearing, this Court may correct that error.

CONCLUSION

The petition for a writ of certiorari should be granted.

Respectfully submitted,

Sonia Grant

Date: 4/23/97

On June 27, 1997.

The Supreme Court of The United S~a=es:

Office of the clerk.

Re: Sonia Grant

v. In Rem Release Board et al.,

No. 96-8803.

The petition for writ of certiorari:

CHAPTER FIVE

This is a story about a Case between Sonia Grant, plaintiff-Appellant and The In Rem Release Board, David N. Dinkins, Mayor, City of New York et al . . . . ., and a Construction Co., Respondents.

About three years ago: On or about, May 24, 1993, Respondents wrongly destroyed my house and personal belongings. Respondents made a mistake with the Block and Lot numbers

Today, Respondents have left bad structural damages to the other adjoining houses.

I brought suit against Respondents several days later, in the Supreme Court of the State of New York, 360 Adams Street, Brooklyn N.Y., Though at the time, I was emotionally distraught. On March 3rd 1994, a decision was made, that, even though her case was compelling, a judgement went for the Respondents; I further took my Case to a Higher Court, the New York State Supreme Court, Appellate Division - Second Department, 45 Monroe Place, Brooklyn N.Y. 11201.

I have overwhelming arguments to win my case and to become vindicated.

I seek the following relief: (a) Prevent the City from performing construction on the Subject Property. (b) Convey Title to Plaintiff. (c) Money Damages. (d) Any other relief the Court may deem proper.

My Case is callendered to be heard in the Appellate Court, Brooklyn N.Y. this Friday, February 23, 1996 at 10 a.m.

Case No.

Transcript of the Meeting of the

IN REM FORECLOSURE RELEASE BOARD

held on Tuesday, July 21, 1992

at City Hall, Borough of Manhattan

Testimony Given by the Following Individuals:

                        Department
                        and Development

                        Representing:
                        Departments

                        Representing:
                        Housing Preservation and Development

                        Representing:
                        S Grant

                        Representinc

Hearing convened at 10:10 a.m.

P R E S E N T:

Mayor's Office of Legislative Affairs

    Assistant Legislative Representative

Speaker of the City Council

Corporation Counsel

    Assistant Corporation Counsel

Comissioner of Finance

    Deputy Commissioner of Operations

President, Borough of the Bronx

President, Borough of Brooklyn

    Assistant to Borough President

President Borough of Manhattan

    Deputy Director for Land Use Planning

Mayor's Office of Contracts Justice delayed is justice denied.

The claim -- First of all, the claim of HPD is that the release should be denied because there are plans for redevelopment of this block and there will be condemnation sometime in the future.

There is no actual plan passed yet. There is no funding. There is an idea. There is a hope. There is a plan.

I plan to retire rich. That doesn't mean anything. With our budget situation we have today in this country, things change. Elections change the face of city government. We don't know what's going to be in two or three or four years when this plan might actually get to the stage where somebody has to vote on whether or not to pass it.

But if the plan -- If the release is denied today, then my client loses the money that she sunk into this house. She loses her home, her children lose their home. And when the city does perhaps condemn this property, they don't have to pay anybody anything.

The building next door was purchased by somebody who is now a real owner, not from the city a private sale. If the property is condemned, the city has to pay that person because that person owns the property and not the City of New York.

Second of all, this has been going on for a couple of years. There have been opportunities in the last two years for this to have been resolved.

However, in 1990, in October of 1990, Ms. Grant received a letter from the Law Department claiming that her application for release, her application for release two years ago, refers to a particular block, which is the actual block of the property. But the letter of the Law Department says that there's a last owner title certification which refers to Block   So   there   was   a mistake made in the title search.

Ms. Grant had to take care of that within a couple of weeks, which she did. But it delayed the process because of an error that had nothing to do with Ms. Grant, had nothing to do with the city. It was a human error.

Then there was -- testifying now.

MR. Our recommendation for denial is based on the fact that one, the property was bought at auction and Ms. Grant defaulted on her two-year repair agreement to repair the property, as well as the fact that she is in default of her purchase money mortgage with the City of New York.

Additionally, the building is located in our Ocean Hill Urban Renewal Area. It is a site included in that urban renewal plan and the building is slated for demolition to allow for new construction of residential property.

It is one of, I believe, three or four buildings that are located there which we have slated for an urban renewal plan and for demolition.

Currently with regard to this urban renewal plan, we are awaiting an EIS study, which is the environmental impact statement, which should take a few months before the ULURP is ready to be submitted.

MR.   When was this plan approved?

MR.   The plan has not been approved yet. we are still at the stage of doing an environmental impact study.   So we have submitted the ULURP yet for approval.   But it should be happening within the next few months.

This is currently adjacent to a new construction site that is located right next door to this particular parcel which is a Section 202 or a senior citizen housing that was recently approved by the City council a few months ago.

MR.   statement that he sent you a letter a year ago to obtain the financing and you never responded to them?

MR.   That is not necessarily accurate.   I have spoken to Ms. Grant on a number of occasions since her application was filed. As you know, our --   Because of the plans of the property, we are recommending a denial at this point.

MS.   Could I put this on second call, please.

MR.   All right, fine.   Put it on second call.

HEARING SECRETARY: Calendar No. 10 is here touring City Hall. throughout the day. I hope you get to see a lot of things in the city.

With that said, Madam Secretary, would you please go on to second call.

HEARING SECRETARY: Second call items, Calendar No. 4.

MR. Calendar No. 4, I'd like to request a layover to the next meeting.

HEARING SECRETARY: Calendar No. 4 will now be laid over to August 11th.

MR. Thank you.

HEARING SECRETARY: Calendar No. 9.

MR. Calendar No. 9, I'd like to close hearing and move the item.

HEARING SECRETARY: Calendar No. 9, on the motion to adopt the resolution denying the release.

Mayor.

MR. Aye.

HEARING SECRETARY: Speaker of the City Council.

MR. Aye.

HEARING SECRETARY: Corporation Counsel.

MS. Aye.

HEARING SECRETARY: Commissioner of Finance.

MR. Aye.

HEARING SECRETARY: President, Borough of Brooklyn.

MS. Aye.

HEARING SECRETARY: Resolution adopted denying the release.

Calendar No. 10.

MR. I'd like to close hearing and move the item on Calendar No. 10.

HEARING SECRETARY: Calendar No. 10, on the motion to adopt the resolution denying the release.

Mayor.

MR. Aye.

HEARING SECRETARY: Speaker of the City Council.

MR. Aye.

HEARING SECRETARY: Corporation Counsel.

MS. Aye.

HEARING SECRETARY: Commissioner of Finance.

MR. Aye.

HEARING SECRETARY: President, Borough of Brooklyn.

MS. Aye.

HEARING SECRETARY: Resolution adopted had denying the release.

Calendar Nos. 11 and 12.

MR.   Calendar Nos. 11 and 12, I'd like to close the hearing and move the items.

HEARING SECRETARY: Calendar Nos. 11 and 12, on the motion to adopt the resolutions denying the release.

Mayor.

MR.   Aye.

HEARING SECRETARY: Speaker of the City Council.

MR.   Aye.

HEARING SECRETARY: Corporation Counsel.

MS.   Aye.

HEARING SECRETARY: Commissioner of Finance.

MR.   Aye.

HEARING SECRETARY: President, Borough of Brooklyn.

Journal:

PRO SE AFFIRM THAT:

- I PURCHASED PROPERTY EASTERN PARKWAY, BROOKLYN, NEW YORK, BLOCK 1473 (THREE STORY) BROWNSTONE BUILDING.

- BOUGHT THIS PROPERTY FOR MYSELF AND MY CHILDREN TO LIVE IN AND OPERATE MY BUSINESS TO WITH NAME:

- WHEN I BOUGHT THIS PROPERTY, I WAS SOLE PURCHASER.

- IMMEDIATELY, AFTER PURCHASING THIS PROPERTY, I STARTED RENOVATION.

- IN 1987, I MOVED INTO MY HOUSE.

- IN MAY OF 1990, WHILE I STARTED NEW RENOVATIONS ON MY HOUSE,

- PROPERTY WOULD BE RELEASED IN FEW MONTHS WITH 4 MONTHS.

- IN JUNE 1992, RECEIVED A LETTER FROM THE IN REM RELEASE BOARD, ON JULY 1992, THE IN REM RELEASE BOARD WILL HOLD A MEETING RELEASE INTEREST IN MY PROPERTY.

- AT THE MEETING ON JULY 1992, (SEE TRANSCRIPT OF MEETING).

- A CONSTRUCTION COMPANY HAS BEGUN ADJOINING MY PROPERTY. TORN DOWN.

- ON THE EVENING OF MAY 1993 I WENT HOME. CONSTRUCTION HAD BROKE INTO MY HOUSE AND STARTED DEMOLITION.

- BY MAY 1993, MY HOUSE WAS TOTALLY DEMOLISHED.

- BEAR THESE STATEMENTS TO BE TRUE AND ASK THE COURT TO RENDER RELIEF.

CHAPTER SIX

SUPREME COURT OF THE STATE OF NEW YORK
COUNTY OF KINGS.

INDEX NO.

SONIA GRANT	PETITIONER

AGAINST

RESPONDENT

IN REM RELEASE BOARD
        MAYOR,CITY OF NEW YORK
        SPEAKER,CORPORATION COUNCIL
COMMISSIONER OF FINANCE,BOROUGH PRESIDENT
HOUSING PRESERVATION AN DEVELOPMENT,
(COMMISSIONER HOUSING PRESERVATION AND DEVELOPMENT)
        CONSTRUCTION,

NOTICE
OF
PETITION

THE 3rd DAY OF ___ SONIA A. GRANT, PRO SE, WILL PETITION THE COURT ON
AT ___ ADAMS ST., BROOKLYN, NY., AT AN IAS
PART TO BE ASSIGNED:

AND WHEREFORE MOVE FOR THE FOLLOWING RELIEF.

A) TO STOP CONSTRUCTION AND EXCAVATION, UNTIL MY CASE
CAN BE RESOLVED.

B) SPECIFIC PERFORMANCE 1-e. IN REM BOARD TO CONVEY
TITLE TO PLAINTIFF.

C) MONEY DAMAGE.

D) ANY OTHER RELIEF TO THIS COURT MAY DEEM PROPER.

C 196—Summons with Notice, Supreme Court.
Personal or Substitute Service. 1-69

© 1973 by JULIUS BLUMBERG, INC.
PUBLISHER, NYC 10013

Supreme Court of the State of New York

County of Kings

S. _ GRANT

IN REM RELEASE BOARD v. e against
　　　　　MAYOR, CITY OF NEW YORK
　　　　　　CORPORATION COUNCIL, BOROUGH
PRESIDENT, COMMISSIONER OF FINANCE, HOUSING
PRESERVATION AND DEVELOPMENT,
　　　　　　　　　　　　CONSTRUCTION.

Plaintiff(s)

Defendant(s)

Index No.

Plaintiff(s) designates
KINGS
County as the place of trial

The basis of the venue is
EASTERN PKWAY
BROOKLYN, NY. 11231

Summons with Notice

Plaintiff(s) reside(s) at
EASTERN PKWAY

County of KINGS

To the above named Defendant(s)

You are hereby summoned to answer the complaint in this action and to serve a copy of your answer, or, if the complaint is not served with this summons, to serve a notice of appearance, on the Plaintiff's Attorney(s) within 20 days after the service of this summons, exclusive of the day of service (or within 30 days after the service is complete if this summons is not personally delivered to you within the State of New York); and in case of your failure to appear or answer, judgment will be taken against you by default for the relief demanded herein.

Dated, May 25th 1993

Defendant's Address:

Attorney(s) for Plaintiff(s) ProSe
Office and Post Office Address

Notice: The nature of this action is illegal Condemnation and Demolition.

The relief sought is TITLE OF PROPERTY TO BE CONVEYED
　　　　　　　　　MONEY DAMAGES -

Upon your failure to appear, judgment will be taken against you by default for the sum of $
with interest from　　　　　　　　　　　　19　　and the costs of this action.

☐ notice of petition and petition   ☐ petition
☐ subpoena   ☐ subpoena duces tecum   ☐ order to show cause
☐

Corporation Council

☒ defendant   } hereinafter
☐ respondent   } called
☐ witness   } the recipient

INDIVIDUAL ☐   by delivering a true copy of each to said recipient personally; deponent knew the person so served to be the person described as recipient therein.

CORPORATION ☒   a DOMESTIC   corporation, by delivering thereat a true copy of each to
personally, deponent knew said corporation so served to be the corporation, described in said recipient and knew said
to be   MANAGING AGENT   (LAW DEPARTMENT)   thereof.

SUITABLE AGE PERSON ☐   by delivering thereat a true copy of each to
age and discretion. Said premises is recipient's ☐ actual place of business ☐ dwelling house (usual place of abode) within

AFFIXING TO DOOR, ETC. ☐   by affixing a true copy of each to the door of said premises, which is recipient's ☐ actual place of business ☐ dwelling house or
☐ abode within the state. Deponent was unable, with due diligence to find recipient or a person of suitable age and discretion
having called there

Deponent talked to   at said premises who stated that recipient ☐ lived ☐ worked

MAILING USE WITH ☐   Deponent caused a copy of same to be enclosed in a postpaid sealed wrapper properly addressed to recipient at recipient's
(3 of 4)   residence, at   and caused said wrapper to be
deposited in a post office—official depository under exclusive care and custody of the U.S. Postal Service within New York State
☐ This mailing was made   within one day after such delivering to each person
or such address ☐ and with return receipt requested.

DESCRIPTION ☐ (1 of 3)	Sex	Color	Hair	Appearance Age	Height	Weight
	☒ Male ☐ Female	☐ White Skin ☒ Black Skin ☐ Yellow Skin ☐ Brown Skin ☐ Red Skin	☒ Black Hair ☐ Brown Hair ☐ Blond Hair ☐ Gray Hair ☐ Red Hair	☐ White Hair ☐ Balding ☒ Mustache ☐ Beard ☐ Glasses	☐ 14-20 Yrs. ☒ 21-35 Yrs. ☐ 36-50 Yrs. ☐ 51-65 Yrs. ☐ Over 65 Yrs.	☐ Under 5' ☐ 5'0"-5'3" ☒ 5'4"-5'8" ☐ 5'9"-6'0" ☐ Over 6'	☐ Under ☐ 100 ☒ 131-1 ☐ 161-1 ☐ Over

Other identifying features:

WITNESS FEES ☐ $ for authorizing travelling expenses and one days' witness fee   ☐ was paid (tendered) to the recipient
☐ was mailed to the witness with sub-

MILITARY SERVICE ☐   I asked the person spoken to whether recipient was in active military service of the United States or of the State of New
capacity whatever and received a negative reply. Recipient wore ordinary civilian clothes and no military uniform. The source of
said and the grounds of my belief are the conversations and observations above narrated.
Upon information and belief I aver that the recipient is not in the military service of New York State or of the United S
terms is defined in either the State or in the Federal statutes.

7/7/9[?]   License No.

Sworn to before me on

TYPE ☐ $ for authorizing travelling expenses and one days' witness fee   ☐ was paid (tendered) to the recipient
☐ was mailed to the witness with subpoena copy

MILITARY SERVICE ☐   I asked the person spoken to whether recipient was in active military service of the United States or of the State of New York in any
capacity whatever and received a negative reply. Recipient wore ordinary civilian clothes and no military uniform. The source of my evidence
said and the grounds of my belief are the conversations and observations above narrated.
Upon information and belief I aver that the recipient is not in the military service of New York State or of the United States as the
term is defined in either the State or in the Federal statutes.

7/8/9[?]   License No.

Sworn to before me on

48

Supreme Court County of Kings

No.

Sonia Grant

Plaintiff(s)/Petitioner(s)

against

AFFIDAVIT
OF
SERVICE

Borough President ET AL

Defendant(s)/Respondent(s)

Kings) COUNTY, NEW YORK STATE:

Deponent is not a party herein, is over 18 years of age and resides in Queens N.Y.

2/17 19 9 J at 11:10AM. at 209 Joralemon St. Bklyn N.Y. 11202

☐ summons and complaint
☐ notice of petition and petition
☐ subpoena   ☐ subpoena duces tecum
☐ citation
☐ order to show cause
☐

Borough President

☒ defendant   ☐ respondent   ☐ witness   called the recipient

by delivering a true copy of each to said recipient personally; deponent knew the person so served to be the person described as recipient therein.

_____ corporation, by delivering thereat a true copy of each to _____ personally, deponent knew said corporation so served to be the corporation, described in same as said recipient and knew said individual to be _____ thereof.

by delivering thereat a true copy of each to _____ a person of suitable age and discretion. Said premises is recipient's ☒ actual place of business ☐ dwelling house (usual place of abode) within the state.

by affixing a true copy of each to the door of said premises, which is recipient's ☐ actual place of business ☐ dwelling house (usual place of abode) within the state. Deponent was unable, with due diligence to find recipient or a person of suitable age and discretion, having called there

Deponent talked to _____ at said premises who stated that recipient ☐ lived ☐ worked

Deponent caused a copy of same to be enclosed in a postpaid sealed wrapper properly addressed to recipient at recipient's last known address, at 209 JORALEMON ST. Bklyn, N.Y. 11202 and caused said wrapper to be deposited in a post office/official depository under exclusive care and custody of the U.S. Postal Service within New York State.

☐ The mailing was made 7/12/93 within one day after such delivery to such person
of such mailing ☐ and with return receipt requested.

Sex	Color	Hair	Approximate Age	Height	Weight
☐ Male	☐ White Skin	☐ Black Hair	☐ White Hair	☐ 14-20 Yrs.	☐ Under 5'	☐ Under
☒ Female	☐ Black Skin	☒ Brown Hair	☐ Balding	☒ 21-35 Yrs.	☐ 5'0"-5'3"	☒ 100-1
	☐ Yellow Skin	☐ Blond Hair	☐ Mustache	☐ 36-50 Yrs.	☒ 5'4"-5'8"	☐ 131-1
	☐ Brown Skin	☐ Gray Hair	☐ Beard	☐ 51-65 Yrs.	☐ 5'9"-6'0"	☐ 14-1
	☐ Red Skin	☐ Red Hair	☐ Glasses	☐ Over 65 Yrs.	☐ Over 6'	☐ Over

Other identifying features:

$ _____ the authorizing travelling expenses and one day's witness fees ☐ was paid (tendered) to the recipient ☐ was mailed to the witness with subpoena

I asked the person spoken to whether recipient was in active military service of the United States or of the State of New York in any capacity whatever and received a negative reply. Recipient wore ordinary civilian clothes and no military uniform. The source of my information and the grounds of my belief are the conversations and observations above narrated. Upon information and belief I aver that the recipient is not in the military service of New York State or of the United States as that term is defined in either the State or in the Federal statutes.

Sworn to before me on

7/13/93

License No.

Supreme Court County of Kings

Sonia Grant

Plaintiff(s)/Petitioner(s)

against

City Of New York ET AL

Defendant(s)/Respondent(s)

No.

AFFID.
OF
SERV

KINGS, County, New York State:

Deponent is not a party herein, is over 18 years of age and resides in Queens N.Y.

On July 6, 19 93 at 4:45 P.M. at 100 Church St New York N.Y.
deponent served the within □ summons □ with notice □ summons, Spanish summons and complaint, the language required by
□ summons and complaint NYCRR 2900.2(e), (f) & (h) was set forth on the face of the summons
□ notice of petition and petition □ citation
□ subpoena □ subpoena duces tecum □ order to show cause

City Of New York □ defendant thereinafter
□ respondent called
□ witness the recipient

<table>
<tr><td>INDIVIDUAL 1. □</td><td>by delivering a true copy of each to said recipient personally; deponent knew the person so served to be the person described as said recipient therein.</td></tr>
<tr><td>CORPORATION 2. □</td><td>a Domestic corporation by delivering thereat a true copy of each to personally, deponent knew said corporation so served to be the corporation, described in same as said recipient and knew said to be Managing Agent thereof</td></tr>
<tr><td>SUITABLE AGE PERSON 3. □</td><td>by delivering thereat a true copy of each to age and discretion. Said premises is recipient's □ actual place of business □ dwelling house (usual place of abode) within</td></tr>
<tr><td>AFFIXING TO DOOR, ETC. 4. □</td><td>by affixing a true copy of each to the door of said premises, which is recipient's □ actual place of business □ dwelling house of abode within the state. Deponent was unable, with due diligence to find recipient or a person of suitable age and discretion having called there</td></tr>
</table>

MAILING
USE WITH
□
(3 or 4)

Deponent talked to at said premises who stated that recipient □ lived □ now
Deponent caused a copy of same to be enclosed in a postpaid sealed wrapper properly addressed to recipient at recipient's
residence, at and caused said wrapper to be
deposited in a post office/official depositary under exclusive care and custody of the U.S. Postal Service within New York State
□ The mailing was made within one day after such delivering to such recipient
at such address □ and with return receipt requested.

DESCRIPTION
□
(or 3)

<table>
<tr><td>Sex</td><td>Color</td><td>Hair</td><td>Approximate Age</td><td>Height</td><td>Weight</td></tr>
<tr><td>☑ Male
□ Female</td><td>□ White Skin
☑ Black Skin
□ Yellow Skin
□ Brown Skin
□ Red Skin</td><td>☑ Black Hair
□ Brown Hair
□ Blond Hair
□ Gray Hair
□ Red Hair</td><td>□ White Hair
□ Balding
☑ Mustache
□ Beard
□ Glasses</td><td>□ 14-20 Yrs.
☑ 21-35 Yrs.
□ 36-50 Yrs.
□ 51-65 Yrs.
□ Over 65 Yrs.</td><td>□ Under 5'
□ 5'0"-5'3"
☑ 5'4"-5'8"
□ 5'9"-6'0"
□ Over 6'</td></tr>
</table>

Other identifying features:

WITNESS
FEES
□

the authorizing travelling expenses and one days' witness fee: □ was paid (tendered) to the recipient
□ was mailed to the witness with

MILITARY
SERVICE
□

I asked the person spoken to whether recipient was in active military service of the United States or of the State of New York in any
capacity whatsoever and received a negative reply. Recipient wore ordinary civilian clothes and no military uniform. The source
tion and the grounds of my belief are the conversations and observations above narrated.
Upon information and belief I aver that the recipient is not in the military service of New York State or of the United
States as defined in either the State or in the Federal statutes.

Sworn to before me on 7/7/93

Signature

Supreme Court County of Kings

Sonia Grant

Plaintiff(s)/Petitioner(s)

Housing Preservation and Development ET AL

Defendant(s)/Respondent(s)

AFFIDAVIT OF SERVICE

KINGS COUNTY, NEW YORK STATE:

July 9, 1993 11:33A. 100 Gold St., New York N.Y.

Housing Preservation And Development

DOMESTIC

MANAGING AGENT

51

1. □ CORPORATION

recipient therein.

corporation, by delivering thereat a true copy of each to

personally, deponent knew said corporation so served to be the corporation, described in same as said recipient and knew said individual to be thereof

2. □ SUITABLE AGE PERSON

a person of suitable

by delivering thereat a true copy of each to

age and discretion. Said premises is recipient's □ actual place of business □ dwelling house (usual place of abode) within the state

3. ☒ AFFIXING TO DOOR, ETC.

by affixing a true copy of each to the door of said premises, which is recipient's □ actual place of business □ dwelling house (usual place of abode) within the state. Deponent was unable, with due diligence to find recipient or a person of suitable age and discretion, thereat having called there

4. □

Deponent talked to   at said premises who stated that recipient □ lived □ worked there

MAILING USE WITH
☑
[3 or 4]

Deponent caused a copy of same to be enclosed in a postpaid sealed wrapper properly addressed to recipient at recipient's last known
____ at   COLD STREET N.Y. N.Y.   and caused said wrapper to
deposited in—a post office—official depository under exclusive care and custody of the U.S. Postal Service within New York State.
□ The mailing was made   JULY 9, 1993   within one day after such delivering to such suitable per-
or such mailing □ and with return receipt requested.

DESCRIPTION
□
(one 3)

Sex	Color	Hair		Approximate Age	Height	Weight
☒ Male	☒ White Skin	□ Black Hair	□ White Hair	□ 14-20 Yrs.	□ Under 5'	□ Under 100 Lbs.
□ Female	□ Black Skin	□ Brown Hair	☒ Balding	□ 21-35 Yrs.	□ 5'0"-5'3"	□ 100-130 Lbs.
	□ Yellow Skin	□ Blond Hair	□ Mustache	□ 36-50 Yrs.	☒ 5'4"-5'8"	☒ 131-160 Lbs.
	□ Brown Skin	□ Gray Hair	□ Beard	☒ 51-65 Yrs.	□ 5'9"-6'0"	□ 161-200 Lbs.
	□ Red Skin	□ Red Hair	☒ Glasses	□ Over 65 Yrs.	□ Over 6'	□ Over 200 Lbs.

Other identifying features:

WITNESS FEES

$ the authorizing travelling expenses and one day's witness fee: □ was paid (tendered) to the recipient
□ was mailed to the witness with subpoena

MILITARY SERVICE
□

I asked the person spoken to whether recipient was in active military service of the United States or of the State of New York in any capacity whatsoever and received a negative reply. Recipient wore ordinary civilian clothes and no military uniform. The source of my information and the grounds of my belief are the conversations and observations above narrated. Upon information and belief I aver that the recipient is not in the military service of New York State or of the United States as that term is defined in either the State or in the Federal statutes.

Sworn to before me on   7/9/93

	□ Brown Skin	☒ Gray Hair	□ Mustache	□ 36-50 Yrs.	☒ 5'4"-5'8"	□ 100-130 Lbs.
	□ Red Skin	□ Red Hair	□ Beard	☒ 51-65 Yrs.	□ 5'9"-6'0"	□ 131-160 Lbs.
			☒ Glasses	□ Over 65 Yrs.	□ Over 6'	☒ 161-200 Lbs.

Other identifying features:

WITNESS FEES
□

$ the authorizing travelling expenses and one day's witness fee: □ was paid (tendered) to the recipient
□ was mailed to the witness with subpoena copy.

MILITARY SERVICE
□

I asked the person spoken to whether recipient was in active military service of the United States or of the State of New York in any capacity whatsoever and received a negative reply. Recipient wore ordinary civilian clothes and no military uniform. The source of my information and the grounds of my belief are the conversations and observations above narrated. Upon information and belief I aver that the recipient is not in the military service of New York State or of the United States as that term is defined in either the State or in the Federal statutes.

Sworn to before me on

License No.

Supreme Court County of Kings

Sonia Grant

Plaintiff(s)/Petitioner(s)

Construction ET AL

Defendant(s)/Respondent(s)

AFFIDAVIT
OF
SERVICE

being sworn

Kings County, New York State.

Deponent is not a party herein, is over 18 years of age and resides at

On JULY 12, 1993 at 3:14 p.M. at BROOKLYN, N.Y.,
BROOKLYN, N.Y.

deponent served the within ☐ summons ☐ with notice

☐ summons, Spanish citation and complaint, the language required by NYCRR 2900.2(e), (f) & (h) was set forth on the face of the summonses

☐ summons and complaint
☐ notice if petition and petition
☐ subpoena ☐ subpoena duces tecum

☐ citation
☐ order to show cause
☐

Scala Construction

☐ defendant
☐ respondent
☐ witness

(hereinafter
called
the recipient)

therein named.

INDIVIDUAL ☐ by delivering a true copy of each to said recipient personally; deponent knew the person so served to be the person described as said recipient therein.

CORPORATION ☒ a DOMESTIC corporation, by delivering thereat a true copy of each to personally, deponent knew said corporation so served to be the corporation, described in same as said recipient and knew said individual to be MANAGING AGENT thereof

SUITABLE AGE PERSON ☐ by delivering thereat a true copy of each to a person of suitable age and discretion. Said premises is recipient's ☐ actual place of business ☐ dwelling house (usual place of abode) within the state.

AFFIXING TO DOOR, ETC. ☐ by affixing a true copy of each to the door of said premises, which is recipient's ☐ actual place of business ☐ dwelling house (usual place of abode) within the state. Deponent was unable, with due diligence to find recipient or a person of suitable age and discretion, thereat, having called there

MAILING USE WITH (3 or 4) ☐ Deponent talked to at said premises who stated that recipient ☐ lived ☐ worked there
Deponent caused a copy of same to be enclosed in a postpaid sealed wrapper properly addressed to recipient at recipient's last known residence, at and caused said wrapper to be deposited in a post office/official depository under exclusive care and custody of the U.S. Postal Service within New York State.
( ) The mailing was made within one day after such delivering to such suitable person
at such mailing ☐ and with return receipt requested.

DESCRIPTION USE WITH (or 3) ☐

Sex	Color	Hair	Approximate Age	Height	Weight
☐ Male	☐ White Skin	☐ Black Hair	☐ White Hair	☐ 14-20 Yrs.	☐ Under 5'	☐ Under 100 Lbs.
☐ Female	☐ Black Skin	☐ Brown Hair	☐ Balding	☐ 21-35 Yrs.	☐ 5'0"-5'3"	☐ 100-130 Lbs.
	☐ Yellow Skin	☐ Blond Hair	☐ Mustache	☐ 36-50 Yrs.	☐ 5'4"-5'8"	☐ 131-160 Lbs.
	☐ Brown Skin	☐ Gray Hair	☐ Beard	☐ 51-65 Yrs.	☐ 5'9"-6'0"	☐ 161-200 Lbs.
	☐ Red Skin	☐ Red Hair	☐ Glasses	☐ Over 65 Yrs.	☐ Over 6'	☐ Over 200 Lbs.

Other identifying features:

WITNESS FEES ☐ $ by authorizing travelling expenses and one days' witness fee: ☐ was paid (tendered) to the recipient
☐ was mailed to the witness with subpoena copy

MILITARY SERVICE ☐ I asked the person spoken to whether recipient was in active military service of the United States or of the State of New York in any capacity whatever and received a negative reply. Recipient wore ordinary civilian clothes and no military uniform. The source of my information and the grounds of my belief are the conversations and observations above narrated.
Upon information and belief I aver that the recipient is not in the military service of New York State or of the United States as the term is defined in either the State or in the Federal statutes.

Sworn to before me on

License No.

53

CHAPTER SEVEN

POINT II

PETITIONER IS BARRED BY THE STATUTE
OF LIMITATIONS FROM CHALLENGING
EITHER THE RESOLUTION OF THE IN REM
FORECLOSURE RELEASE BOARD OR THE
CITY'S RIGHT TO EXCAVATE THE SUBJECT
PROPERTY

Notwithstanding the reasons previously proffered, the instant petition must be dismissed as petitioner's challenge to the Release Board's determination is barred by the statute of limitations. Since the relief petitioner requests in the Summons with Notice is the same relief requested in the Petition, and because the challenged action is to a governmental body's decision, plaintiff's action constitutes a special proceeding under Article 78 of the CPLR. An Article 78 proceeding is "the customary procedural vehicle for review of administrative determinations." Solnick v. Whalen, 49 NY2d 224, 231 (1980).

The law is well settled that any challenge to an administrative body's decision must be commenced within four months. CPLR 217 provides that "a proceeding against a body or officer must be commenced within four months after the determination to be reviewed becomes final and binding upon petitioner..." Accordingly, petitioner's challenge to the July 21, 1992 resolution of the Release Board which petitioner commenced on or about July 6, 1993 is time barred by eight months.

Thus, the presumption In Admin. Code 5 11-412(c) operates as a two-year Statute of Limitations. Matter of ISCA Enterprises v. City of New York, 160 Ad2d 698, 699 (2d Dept., 1990), affirmed, 77 NY2d 688, 697 (1991),cert. denied, 112 S.Ct. 1263 (1992); Matter of Tax Foreclosure No. 35, 127 AD2d 220, 228 (2d Dept., 1987), affirmed, 71 NY2d 863 (1988). Therefore, petitioner's challenge to the City's ownership of the subject property commenced on or about July 6, 1993 is time barred by approximately thirteen months.

In sum, petitioner's challenges to the resolution of the Release Board and to the City's right to ownership of the subject property are time barred, and as petitioner has not alleged and has not shown fraud or illegality in the Release Board's denial of petitioner's application, the Board's determination should not be disturbed and the order appealed from should be affirmed.

CONCLUSION
THE ORDER APPEALED FROM SHOULD BE AFFIRMED.

SUPREME COURT OF THE STATE OF NEW YORK
COUNTY OF KINGS.

INDEX NO.

SONIA   GRAFF   PETITIONER

AGAINST

IN REM RELEASE BOARD   ANSWER
        MAYOR,CITY OF NEW YORK   AGAINST
        SPEAKER,CORPORATION COUNCIL   CROSS
COMMISSIONER OF FINANCE,BOROUGH PRESIDENT   MOTION TO
HOUSING PRESERVATION AN DEVELOPMENT,   DISMISS
(COMMISSIONER HOUSING PRESERVATION AND DEVELOPMENT)
        CONSTRUCTION.
                                    RESPONDENT

Please Take Notice that   dated
August   1993, Petitioner in this suit, will move this Court, at
an IAS part - thereof, to be held at the Court house located at
360 adams street, against Defendants Cross Motion to dismiss on
the grounds that it is barred by the statue of limitations.

PLEASE TAKE NOTICE, That, Petitioner's answer against
Defendant's Cross Motion to dismiss is on the following reasons:

Journal:

.- On February   1985, Petitioner purchased Property
Eastern Parkway, Brooklyn, New York, Block 1473   (three
story) Brownstone Building Located at the Corner of Eastern
Parkway and Howard Ave.

.- In May of 1990, Petitioner received a letter from the City,
  saying that her property was In Rem for back taxes.
  Print Out is annexed hereto as Exhibit

-.- On July   1990 Petitioner paid all her taxes owed.
    Petitioner
    (Her receipts for payment of taxes).

.- On or about July   1990 Petitioner applied for a Mandatory
  .Release of the City's Interest in her Property, because

56

Petitioner paid all her taxes within four months of the City's acquisition. Petitioner's application was approved.

2.- On or about, July   1990, Petitioner was told, by the City at 2 Lafayette Street, to wait a few months for her release papers.

City's Acquisition of Title to the Subject Property.

3.- On or about, July   1990, Petitioner did a Title search on her Property. A copy of Title search is annexed hereto as Exhibit

Petitioner must not be Time - Barred From Challenging the Validity of the City's Title.

4.- On or about, November 1990, as Petitioner waited for her release papers, as she was told.
Petitioner received a letter from the City's Law Department, saying that they made a mistake with Petitioner's Block and Lot number, and that Petitioner should come into their office to help them correct the block and lot number (a copy of the November 1990 letter is annexed hereto as exhibit   )

5.- Defendant refers to a March   1991, letter,

Petitioner's application was approved:

6.- On or about, June 1992, Petitioner received a letter, saying hat her application for the release of the City's Interest will appear before an in rem release board on July 21, 1992. A copy of the June 1992 letter is annexed hereto as Exhibit

7.- On July 21, 1992, the meeting was held. During the meeting the Board called for a "holdover" on Petitioner Property.

8.- At the second round of the meeting. Some voted Yes, and some voted No.

9.-
Petitioner never heard from the Board, nor the City.

NEW YORK SUPREME COURT

Appellate Division - Second Department

------------- Case. No.

In The Matter of Application

of

S   Grant,

Plaintiff - Appellant,

against

In Rem Release **Board,** ..   Mayor,

City of New York, et al   ,

Construction.

.... Respondents.

PLAINTIFF- APPELLANT'S BRIEF

November   1994.

S   Grant, (PROSE)

Plaintiff- Appellant

SUPREME COURT OF THE STATE OF NEW YORK

APPELLATE DIVISION: SECOND DEPARTMENT.

In the Matter of the Application of

  S Grant,   Case. No.

Plaintiff- Appellant,

-against-

In Rem Release Board,   Mayor,

City of New York,   Speaker,

Corporation Council, Commissioner of Finance, Borough President,

Housing Preservation and Development, (Commissioner Housing

Preservation and Development.)

    Construction.

Statement Under Rule 5531

1. The index Number assigned in the Court below is 17342/93.

2. The full names of the original parties are set forth above. There has been no change of parties since the commencement of this action.

3. This special proceeding was commenced in Supreme Court of the State of New York.

4. This special proceeding was commenced by the Service of a Notice of Retition and Petition on or about May 1993. Respondent's Verified Answer and Return was served on or about June 1993.

5. The nature and object of this special proceeding pursuant to CPLR Article 78 was to challenge the right of the City to construct upon and / or excavate the subject property, to compel the City of New York to convey title to the property to Plaintiff and for money damages.

6. The court below determined that this determination was not arbitrary or capricious nor was it an abuse of discretion.

7. The appeal is on full reproduced record.

8. The determination to be reviewed was rendered after reading the notice of cross-motions and after due deliberation having been held thereon.

Questions Involved

Statements of Facts and Nature of the case

Argument

Point 1   Whether the actions taken
           by respondents were in conformity of the law

Point 11   Whether respondents are liable for negligence,
           trespass, destruction and wrongful demolition of
           Plaintiff's property

Conclusion: THE ACTIONS TAKEN BY RESPONDENTS
                 WERE NOT IN CONFORMITY OF THE LAW;
                 AND PLAINTIFF PROPERLY REDEEMED HER
                 INTEREST IN HER PROPERTY

CHAPTER EIGHT

Questions involved

1. Whether the actions taken by respondents were in conformity of the law.

   The Court below did not answer this question.

2. Whether Plaintiff properly redeemed her interest in her property

   The Court below did not answer this question.

3. Whether respondents are liable for negligence, trespass; destruction and wrongful demolition of Plaintiff's property.

   The Court below did not answer this question.

On October 1990, Plaintiff received a letter from the City's law department, to say that, the release of her property was in defect, because her application for release of her property refers to Block 1473 and last owner title certification refers to Block 1474 that she referred to. (See copy of this letter. Exhibit B.)

Is it a matter, that the City made a mistake.

Upon request, Plaintiff presented to the City's law department, a certification, which certifies Plaintiff's block (See exhibit C.)

In June 1992, Plaintiff received another letter to say that, An In REM Board will hold a meeting to release interest in Plaintiff's property

At that meeting, on July 1992, the In Rem Board voted not to release interest in Plaintiff's property, without giving any substantiable reason.

On May   1993 through May 1993. The City and
Construction destroyed Plaintiff's house and all her
belongings, without any Notice.

Point 1

Whether the actions taken by respondents were in
conformity of the law.

   Respondents contend that Plaintiff merely applied, in July
1990, for release of muncipal respondents interest in her
property; and respondents contend that, according to Chapter 4
of Title 11 of the Administrative Code of New York, respondents
acted within the law; and that respondents further contend that,
Plaintiff's release of muncipal interest in her property was
subject to payment of charges in an April 1991 letter; which
Plaintiff contends that, she never received any such letter.
Respondents further contend that Plaintiff could not meet the
deadline of the April 1991, which was stated in that letter; and
because of her indebtedness and by resolution dated July 1992.
Respondents destroyed Plaintiff's house.

Point II

Whether respondents are liable for negligence, trespass,
destruction and wrongful demolition of Plaintiff's
property.

   In Hogan v Alabama Power Co. The Court held; Since Jury,s
verdict in favor of landlord was not inadequate when viewed as
award of damages for trespass, court could not consider appeal
contention that the award was inadequate under the Statute
dealing with damages for wrongfully and knowingly cutting
timber. (Code of Ala. Tit. 47 § 272 - Hoaan v Alabama Power Co.)

Plaintiff in the case contends that her house was a Sound 3 family attached Brownestone House, (Picture of Plaintiff's house annexed hereto as Exhibit D.) and that on the day of May 1993, The City of New York and Scala Construction began to destroy Plaintiff's property and by May 27, 1993, Plaintiff's property and her belongings were totally destroyed. After Plaintiff thoroughly interrogated, Construction workmen; the workmen told Plaintiff that they had broken into Plaintiff's in order to demolish Plaintiff's house.

Plaintiff further contends that, Construction in the act of demolishing Plaintiff's house, has caused extreme structural damage to the property, right and adjoining of Plaintiff's property;

Plaintiff and her family still suffers loss and injuries of personal and property damages, bereavement and emotional distress.

Plaintiff seeks, a) prevent the City from performing construction on the Subject Property.

b) Convey Title to Plaintiff.

c) money damages

d) Any other relief to this Court may deem proper.

Discussion and Conclusion.
Should Plaintiff be entitled to have a fair and just trial

It is fair to say, that historically, the Courts have been silent and inactive in certain reform process, Society has great confidence in the statutes and uniform acts and many of them have done much good.

Unfortunately, Some courts act mindlessly because the "law" requires it. The law also requires balance, proportion, compassion and decency. Judges should refer to these concerns more often when reaching their decisions.

When society, through the courts, looks at the question of fiduciary Administration, it should not be a fuzzy formalist.

For example, in some jurisdictions, if a trust does not contain the magic word "apply" the trustee cannot make payments on the account of an incompetent beneficiary, and the court must appoint a guardian to receive money and spend it.

Intent, fairness, impartiality and efficiency are the very essence of trust administration. Not to make them the of every case that must give a voice to the silence is unfortunate, to undermine a trust on the basis of silence is regrettable.

Courts find impartiality in every silent trust, and they can as easily find a call for common sense, modernity, and the best rule available-The current practice is backwards.

SUPREME COURT OF THE STATE OF NEW YORK
APPELLATE DIVISION: SECOND DEPARTMENT

---x

In the Matter of S Grant,

NOTICE OF

MOTION

Appellant,

-against-

In Rem Release Board,   Mayor,
City of New York, et al.,

Appellate
Division
Case Number

Respondents.

---x

SIR OR MADAM:

PLEASE TAKE NOTICE, that upon the annexed affirmation
of Appellant, in this case, the annexed exhibits and prior
memorandum of Law, in and prior proceedings herein, the
undersigned will move this Court, at the Courthouse, at
Brooklyn, New York, on August 1996, at 9:30 a.m or soon
thereafter as counsel may be heard, for an order granting LEAVE
TO APPEAL TO THE COURT OF APPEALS.

WHEREFORE, Plaintiff-
Appellant respectfully requests that the Court grant the relief
sought in the above motion and such other and further relief as
the Court deems just and proper.

Dated: New York, New York

August 1996

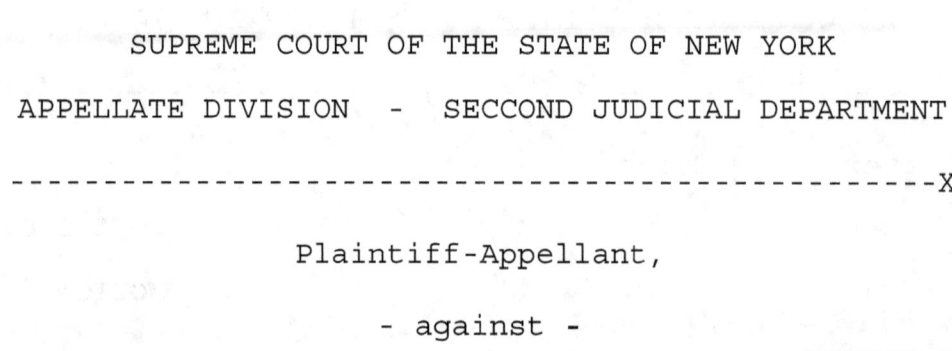

SUPREME COURT OF THE STATE OF NEW YORK

APPELLATE DIVISION - SECCOND JUDICIAL DEPARTMENT

---X

Plaintiff-Appellant,

- against -

MOTION TO
STRIKE THE
BRIEF.

IN REM RELEASE BOARD,   MAYOR
CITY OF NEW YORK, et al.,
        CONSTRUCTION.

Case No.

Respondents-Respondents.

---X

Sirs:

Please take Notice that, Plaintiff, Appellant, in this case, move this Court, at the Courthouse, Brooklyn, New York to Strike Respondents'Brief; providing good cause shown in this motion.

Plaintiff- Appellant, perfected her brief on November 1994, and set forth in her brief overwhelming evidence and facts to support her case. Respondents' Brief of December 1995 is untimely: Lack of proper evidence and facts, fairness, and a Breech of the Statue of Limitations.

Respondents,   after   wrongfully   demolishing   Plaintiff-Appellant's house, took over one year to Respond to my brief. Respondents should not use Statue of limitations to mock the Court, instead should look into this case with due respect and seriousness. Respondents had more than sufficient time to reply to my brief, of November 1994; which shows on Respondents' part; guilt, a lack of concern and seriousness towards my case. In

Addition, the Court would have had sufficient time to Calendar my case,

Therefore, Plaintiff- Appellant, am asking the Court to Strike Respondents' Brief; and if my Motion is not granted, I am asking for time to file a reply brief.

Wherefore, Plaintiff-Appellant, bear these statements to be true; and ask that Motion be granted.

_____

Dated: New York, New York.
January 1996.

CHAPTER NINE

SUPREME COURT OF THE STATE OF NEW YORK
APPELLATE DIVISION: SECOND DEPARTMENT
IN THE MATTER OF S GRANT,

                             Appellant,

        - against -

IN REM RELEASE BOARD, ET AL.,

                         Respondents.

                                AFFIRMATION IN SUPPORT
                                MOTION FOR REARGUMENT,
                                RENEWAL, OR LEAVE TO
                                APPEAL TO THE COURT OF
                                APPEALS

                                Appellate Division
                                Case Number

Appeals.

3. This affirmation is submitted in support of appellant's motion for reargument, renewal, or leave to appeal to the Court of Appeals.

4. This Court decided appellant's appeal by order dated April 1, 1996 (see Exhibit A). In that order, this Court affirmed the granting of summary judgment to the respondents.

Factual Background

5. In 1985, appellant bought the building at Eastern Parkway, Brooklyn (Section 5, Block 1473,), from the City of New York

(the "City"), at a city auction. The building was a three-family residence.

6. Appellant moved into the building in 1986

7. According to the City, appellant fell behind in her payment of taxes, and the City brought a foreclosure action against the property (In Rem Tax Foreclosure .Action No. 37, Borough of Brooklyn index No.

10. On July 1990, the appellant applied for release of the property pursuant to Administrative Code section 11424 and paid the amounts due (Whether appellant paid the full amount due on that date or merely applied for release and paid a deposit on the amount due is a matter of dispute. Resolution of that dispute is not necessary for decision on this motion or the claims that appellant is pursuing in this motion.)

11. By letter dated October 1990, from the Law Department's In Rem Section to appellant, the City incorrectly asserted to appellant that her application for release of the property referred to Block 1473, when "Last owner Title Certification refers to Block 1474"
(Exhibit B). In fact, appellant had correctly referred to Block 1473, as the subject of the application.

12. By letter dated March 1991, the City listed the amounts allegedly due before it would return the property to appellant

and asserted that in order for appellant to be entitled to mandatory release of the property, she would be required to pay those amounts, in full, by April 1991.

13. By application dated April 1991, appellant asked to be permitted to pay those amounts in installments.

14. Over a year later, by letter dated June 1992, the City notified appellant that her application for release would appear before the In Rem Foreclosure Release Board on June 1992.

15. The matter actually appeared before the Board on July 21, 1992. At that proceeding, an attorney testified for appellant and appellant also testified. At the conclusion of the meeting, the Board voted to deny appellant's motion for an installment agreement to gain release of the property.

16. On May 1993, the City notified respondent it had cleared several buildings for demolition, including Contracting Co., Inc. (   ) that Eastern Parkway. The notice that the City gave and provided that demolition was to begin within ten working days. It also provided that to obtain and display the demolition permits for the buildings it had contracted to demolish (Exhibit C).

17. At that time, appellant still lived in the building, still had all of her personal belongings there, and had telephone service in the building. Further, appellant still maintained

security in the building, locking the doors and otherwise taking action designed to exclude intruders.

18. To all outward appearances, the building was being used as a residence.

19. never posted the required demolition notice outside appellant's home. Neither the City nor   notified appellant that it was planning to demolish appellant's home before the actual demolition work began No notice to quit, pursuant to Real Property Actions and Proceedings Law sections 713 and 735, was ever served upon appellant.

20. One evening later that month of May 1993, appellant returned home to find on the block. She was told that her home was the next to be demolished. The next day, appellant returned in the process of demolishing her home. Within a day, appellant's home was completely demolished, and her personal property within the home was completely destroyed.

Proceedings After Demolition

21. In either the Spring or Summer of 1993. appellant, proceeding pro se filed suit in the Supreme Court, Kings Count, seeking I) to enjoin construction and excavation of the lot on which her house had stood; 2) title to the lot; 3) monetary damages and 4) any other relief that the court considered proper (see Notice of Petition, annexed hereto as Exhibit).

22. On July 1993, appellant filed a Notice of Claim with the City alleging: wrongful demolition of her home; negligence; trespass; destruction of her personal property; conversion; property damage; severe emotional distress and personal injuries; and de facto condemnation of real and personal property. Appellant claimed damages for destruction of her home, for her personal property, damages for personal injury and emotional distress (Exhibit).

23. The respondent filed answers and sought dismissal of the suit on the merits and also on procedural grounds

24. By decision dated November 1993 (Exhibit), the lower court granted respondents' motions for summary judgment. in the nature of an Article 78 proceeding (see C.P.L.IL § 7801 et seq.), redeem appellant's roterest tn he building

The court did not rule on that aspect of the suit that claimed monetary damages.

25. By Order dated March 1994, the lower court dismissed appellant's suit (Exhibit).

26. On April 1994, appellant filed a Notice of Appeal (Exhibit).

27. On or about November 1994, after various proceedings in this Court relating to poor-person status, appellant, still proceeding pro se, perfected her appeal. The City filed a

respondent's brief on or about December 1995, and the case was argued on February, 1996.

28. By decision and order dated April 1996, this Court affirmed the lower court's dismissal of appellant's suit and held that the respondent City's denial of appellant's application for an installment agreement was neither arbitrary nor capricious because appellant failed to demonstrate that the In Rem Foreclosure Release Board had acted fraudulently or illegally (Grant v. In Rem Release Board, No. 94-03574 (2d Dep't Apr. 1, 1996). The Court did not address that portion of appellant's suit that sought monetary damages.

29. Because the lower court addressed only those equitable claims cognizable on an Article 78 proceeding and failed to address any of appellant' s legal claims for monetary damages, its decision to dismiss the entire case was erroneous (see accompanying Memorandum of Law). For the same reason, this Court's decision affirming the lower court's decision was also erroneous.

30. Further, respondents' arguments with respect to the statute of limitations, raised both in the lower court and in this Court, clearly do not apply to the claims regarding destruction of personal property and infliction of emotional distress, because appellant raised her claims of such damage

within days of the destruction of the building in which appellant was living. Thus, dismissal on statute of limitaUons grounds would not be the inevitable result if this Court were to grant rearmament and renewal of the appeal.

WHEREFORE, for the reasons stated above, and in the Memorandum of Law, appellant's motion for reargument or leave to appeal to the Court of Appeals should be granted.

Dated: May 1996

New York, New York

CHAPTER TEN

SUPREME COURT OF THE STATE OF NEW YORK
APPELLATE DIVISION: SECOND DEPARTMENT

IN THE MATTER OF S GRANT,
                        Appellant,

        - against -

IN REM RELEASE BOARD, ET AL.,
                        Respondents.

AFFIRMATION IN SUPPORT
MOTION FOR REARGUMENT,
RENEWAL, OR LEAVE TO
APPEAL TO THE COURT OF
APPEALS

Appellate Division
Case Number

ARGUMENT

THE LOWER COURT, IN GRANTING SUMMARY
JUDGMENT, AND THIS COURT, IN AFFIRMING THE
LOWER COURT'S DECISION, OVERLOOKED THAT
PORTION OF APPELLANT'S SUIT SEEKING MONETARY
DAMAGES IN TORT.

In her suit, appellant originally sought the return of real estate pursuant to the City's redemption procedures (see N.Y.C. Admin. Code § 11-424 et seq.), monetary damages for destruction of the building on that property, and monetary damages for destruction of her personal property and for infliction of emotional distress based on the demolition of the house in which she was living. Although appellant, proceeding pro se until now, did not plead her causes of action with the particularity expected of an attorney, her allegations were sufficient to raise claims in tort. Nevertheless, in responding to appellant's allegations, the City addressed only that portion of her claims seeking to overturn the In Rem Review Board's decision rejecting appellant's application to be permitted to pay back taxes and delinquency charges in installments. Likewise, the lower court and this Court addressed only the claims cognizable in an Article 78 proceeding. Because there are [actual issues in dispute relating to appellant's tort claims, and those claims exist independently of the claims cognizable in Article 78 proceedings, summary, judgment should not have been granted. Therefore. reargument should be granted, the lower court's decision granting summary judgment to the respondents should be reversed, and the case should be remitted for further proceedings.

A motion for reargument is proper where a court "overlooked or misapprehended the facts or law or for some reason mistakenly arrived at its earlier decision."

Motions for reargument are addressed to the sound discretion of the court. <u>Id</u>. In this case, facts appearing in appellant's initial papers were sufficient to raise <u>an issue</u> in tort, and both the lower court and this Court overlooked that issue in their decisions. (Appellant's motion for reargument, renewal, or leave to appeal to the Court of Appeals does not address the validity of the foreclosure and refusal to release the property to appellant. This motion is addressed solely to appellant's claims in tort, which neither this Court nor the lower court addressed.) Moreover, a motion for renewal is proper where the moving party alleges new facts. Because appellant is also presenting new facts in this motion, it is also denominated as one for renewal.

Appellant's pro se allegations raised issues of fact that were sufficient to withstand a motion for summary judgment. It is well-settled that on a motion for summary judgment, the papers should be "scrutinized carefully in the light most favorable to the party opposing the motion."

Summary judgment should be granted "only if there are no material and triable issues of fact." Id.

In her Summons and Notice, appellant described the nature of the action as "illegal condemnation and demolition" (see Exhibit). In her Notice of Petition (also contained in Exhibit), appellant asked, in addition to her requests for injunctive and equitable relief, for money damages

Among the facts appellant alleged in support of her request was that on the evening of May 1993, she went home and was told

that her home was "next to be torn down." The next day,
appellant's home and demolished the building, along with
appellant's personal property.

These allegations were sufficient to establish a claim in
tort, or at least to alert the court and the respondents of a
claim in tort, regardless of the validity of appellant's claims
with respect to her ownership of the building. Indeed, given
appellant's continued residence in the building up to the tune
of its demolition, and the presence in the building of all of
her personal belongings and effects, the City had a duty to
appellant to give her sufficient notice of the impending
demolition of the building so that appellant could take legal
action to enjoin its destruction or, at the very least, to
remove her belongings.

Instead, the respondents' destruction of the property left
appellant without a place and without any of her property.
(Appellant's entitlement to damages for destruction of her
personal property and for emotional distress exists
independently of her right to be restored to possession of the
real property. Thus, even if the court below was correct in
dismissing that part of her suit that sought return of the real
property, it was wrong in dismissing the entire suit.)

Even assuming, but without conceding, that the City was the lawful owner of the building and that appellant had no rights as an owner, she still should have been free from the gratuitous destruction of her personal property within the building. With little effort or delay, the could have utilized a summary proceeding by serving a ten-day notice to quit, without destroying appellant's personal property. Instead, despite no need for quick action -- as of early 1996, the lot was still empty -- the respondents elected to demolish the building containing all of appellant's personal property and effects without giving appellant notice to quit. The forcible destruction of appellant's property entitled appellant to recovery of treble damages pursuant to Real Property Actions and Proceedings Law.

Appellant's claims in tort do not depend on her legal status with respect to the property. Whether she was the owner of the property, a tenant, a licensee, or even a trespasser, the City owed her a duty not to inflict intentional harm on her or her property. Given her open and assertive residence in the property, the City's destruction of it, without giving her sufficient notice to remove her property was actionable as an intentional, or perhaps, as a negligent destruction of her personal property, and as an intentional or negligent infliction of emotional distress. <u>See Nieves v. 331 East 109th Street Corp.,</u> 112 A.D.2d 59 (1st Dep't 1985).

In sum, appellant raised sufficient claims below to have withstood a motion for summary judgment, at least with respect to appellant's claims in tort. The lower court therefore erred in granting summary judgment to respondents and dismissing the entire suit. It is apparent from this Court's decision that it did not consider the propriety of the lower court's decision as it pertained to appellant's tort claims. By granting reargument or renewal, this Court may correct that error.

CONCLUSION

This Court should either grant appellant's motion for reargument or renewal, in which event it should reverse the order appealed from and remand to the lower court for further proceedings, or it should grant appellant permission to appeal to the Court of Appeals.

Dated: May 1996
         New York, New York

                                    for Appellant

SUPREME COURT OF THE STATE OF NEW YORK
APPELLATE DIVISION: SECOND DEPARTMENT

IN THE MATTER OF S GRANT,

                    Appellant,

        - against -

IN REM RELEASE BOARD, ET AL.,

MAYOR, CITY OF NEW YORK, ET AL.,
                    Respondents.

AFFIRMATION IN SUPPORT
MOTION FOR REARGUMENT,
RENEWAL, OR LEAVE TO
APPEAL TO THE COURT OF
APPEALS

Appellate Division
Case Number

Plaintiff- Appellant in this suit, affirms the truth of the following statements.

1. This affirmation is submitted in support of appellant's motion for leave to appeal to the Court of Appeals.

2. This Court decided appellant's appeal by order dated April 1996 (Exhibit). In that order, this Court affirmed the granting of summary judgement to respondents on the basis of the lower Court's decision.

3. The lower Court seems wrong as it overlooked or misapprehended the matter of facts or law presented in this case.

4. This Court's decision seems wrong as it also overlooked or misapprehended the facts or law, overlooked by the lower Court.

5. By decision and order dated April 1996, this Court affirmed the lower court's decision of appellant's suit and held that, once the four-month period expired and the appellant failed to pay the outstanding taxes and other charges due on the property within 30 days of the letter requesting her to do so, the release of the property became discretionary rather than mandatory (Grant V In Rem Release Board (2nd Dep't Apr. 1, 1996): This is erroneous and the Court's decision is wrong. This Court overlooked and misinterpreted that portion of fact and law in appellant's suit.

6. The four-month period did not expire: In fact, Appellant paid the outstanding taxes within the four-month period which entitled her to a mandatory release of her property (Exhibit), and the letter referred to; and requesting the appellant to pay outstanding taxes and other charges, within 30 days of the date is erroneous and misinterpretation of the facts and law (Exhibit).

7. Appellant did not fail to act reasonably in protecting her own interests. In fact, because, appellant acted within the four-month period, appellant is entitled to a mandatory release,

Thus respondents constructively, intentionally and fraudulently denied appellant of the return of her property and by process, respondents unlawfully conviscated and intentionally destroyed appellant's property; causing tremendous impact of infliction of mental and emotional distress to appellant.

8. Through constructive, intentional fraud and illegality, respondents violated appellant's human and constitutional rights.

9. Further, appellant's arguments with respect regarding destruction of real property and infliction of emotional distress and damages, raised within days of the destruction of the building in which appellant was living, was raised both in the lower court and in this Court, is a result of the impact of respondents bureaucratic snafu and constructive fraud and illegality.

10. On May 1996, appellant submitted a motion for reargument of an appeal. This Court denied the motion.

WHEREFORE, for the reasons stated above, and in annexed exhibits, appellants motion for leave to appeal to the Court of Appeals on constitutional grounds should be granted.

Dated: August   1996

New York, New York

_____

Sonia Grant (Pro Se)

Sonia, Grant, PRose

Appellant .

V.

_In Rem Release Board, David N. Dinkins,
Mayor, City of New York et al.,_
Respondents

Index No. _____
County **KINGS**

    i. This Motion for Permission to Appeal to the Court of Appeals is being made by _Prose, Appellant_ .

The return date is _____

    ii. The questions presented for Court of Appeals review are:

1. Whether through intentional fraud and illegality, respondents unlawfully conviscated appellants property and violated appellant's human and constitutional rights?
2. Whether respondents are liable for negligence, trespass, destruction and wrongful demolition of Plaintiffs property?
3. Whether the actions taken by respondents were in conformity of the law?
4. Whether respondents are liable to the State of New York?
5. Whether its a matter of race?
6. Whether appellant has the right to a fair trial?

    iii. The order which I am appealing was (circle one) (mailed) personally served upon me by the opposing party with notice of entry on _April 1, 1996_ .
(A copy of this order and opinion must be attached to these papers)

    If you made a motion for permission to this Court in the Appellate Division, you must complete the statements in the box and attach a copy of the order denying your motion with notice of entry to these papers. If no such motion was first made in the Appellate Division go to paragraph iv on the next page.

> the date that I (circle one) (mailed)/
> personally served the Appellate Division motion
> upon the opposing side was _May 24, 1996 / August 30, 1996_
>
> the date that the Appellate Division order
> denying the motion and notice of its entry
> were (circle one) (mailed)/personally served upon me by the opposing party was
> _May 3, 1996 / October 2, 1996_

iv. The Court of Appeals has jurisdiction to review this order because

Respondents violated appellant's human and constitutional rights, through constructive, intentional fraud and illegality. The lower court's decision to dismiss the entire case was erroneous. The Appellate court's decision affirming lower court's decision was also erroneous and wrong.

v. The Court of Appeals should accept this case for review because

The Appellate Court's decision seems wrong as it overlooked or misapprehended the facts or law, overlooked by the lower court. The Appellate Court overlooked and misinterpreted that portion of fact and law in appellant's suit. The Appellate's Courts decision is erroneous and wrong. Appellant's arguments with respect regarding destruction of real property and infliction of emotional distress and damages, raised within days of the destruction of the building in which appellant was living, was raised both in the lower court and in the Appellate court is a result of the impact of respondents fraud and illegality

(use additional sheets if necessary)

SUPREME COURT
OF UNITED STATES

--------------------------------x

        Petitioner,
   v.

In Rem Release Board et al.,

    Construction Co., Inc.

      Respondents.

--------------------------------x

AFFIRMATION IN

SUPPORT OF

PETITION FOR

REHEARING.
No. 95-8803

ARGUMENT

THE LOWER COURT, IN GRANTING SUMMARY
JUDGEMENT, AND THE APPELLATE COURT,
IN AFFIRMING THE LOWER COURTS DECISION,
OVERLOOKED THAT PORTION OF PETITIONER'S
SUIT SEEKING MONETARY DAMAGES IN TORT.

In petitioner's suit, petitioner originally sought the return
of real estate pursuant to the City's redemption procedures (see
N.Y.C. Admin. Code 11- 424 et seq.), monetary damages for
destruction of the building on that property, and monetary
damages for destruction of the building on that property, and
monetary damages for destruction of her personal property and
for infliction of emotional distress based on the demolition of
the house in which she was living. Because there are factual
issues in dispute relating to petitioner's tort claims, and
those claims exist independently of the claims cognizant in

Article 78 proceedings. Summary judgement in the lower court should not have been granted. Therefore, rehearing should be granted, the lower court's decision granting summary judgement to the City and Scala should be reversed, and the case should be remitted for rehearing.

The rehearing for petition is proper where a court "overlooked or misapprehended the facts or law or for some reason mistakenly arrived at its earlier decision." Swenning v. Wankel, 140 A.D. 2d 428 (2d Dep't 1988). Moreover, a petition for rehearing is proper where the moving party alleges new facts. Petitioner raised issues of fact that are substantial to withstand a petition for rehearing. Refer to Rule 44, SUPREME COURT OF THE UNITED STATES.

Petitioner's petition for the rehearing is substantial to establish a claim in tort, or at least to alert the court and the respondents of a claim in tort, regardless of the validity of petitioner's claims with respect to her ownership of the building. Even assuming, but not conceding, that the City was the lawful owner of the building and that petitioner had no rights as the owner, petitioner still should have been free from the gratuitous destruction of personal property within the building. Instead, no need for quick action, as of the present, July 1997, the lot is still empty. The forcible destruction of petitioner's property entitled petitioner to recovery of treble damages pursuant to Real Property Actions and Proceedings Law

Section 853 (Action for forcible or unlawful entry or detainer; treble damages).

Petitioner's claim in tort do not depend on petitioner's legal status with respect to the property. Whether petitioner was the owner of the property, a tenant, a licensee, or even a trespasser, the City owed petitioner a duty not to inflict intentional harm on petitioner or petitioner's property.

In sum, petitioner raises substantial grounds in her petition for rehearing, even with respect to petitioner's claims in tort. The lower court therefore erred in granting 3ummary judgement to respondents and dismissing the entire 3uit. The Appellate's Court's decision did not consider the propriety of the lower court's decision as it pertained to petitioner's tort claims. By granting a petition for the rehearing, this Court may correct that error.

ABOUT THE AUTHOR

I am currently a high school teacher. In my spare time, I write several journal articles and editorials. My recent experience motivated me to expand my writing to novels. I have a copyright for my story, A Client's Point of View.

I would like the opportunity to dedicate this book to my family, friends, my three children, and my parents.

www.ingramcontent.com/pod-product-compliance
Lightning Source LLC
Chambersburg PA
CBHW081223280526
45787CB00006B/2504